INFINITY STANDING UP

by
Drew
Pisarra

Published by Capturing Fire Press, Washington, DC

ISBN: 978-1-7328759-1-3

Capturing Fire Press is an independent publishing house founded by Regie Cabico that seeks to promote politically charged, performance & experimental poetry of the highest quality by diverse queer poets from around the globe.

Copyright 2019 by Capturing Fire Press
All rights reserved. No part of this book may be reproduced, scanned, or distributed in any printed or electronic form without permission of the publisher or the author. All inquired and permissions requests should be addressed to the publisher at **capfirepress@gmail.com**.

Printed in the United States of America

Front and back cover designs and photography by Molly Gross

TABLE OF CONTENTS

Foreword (But Not Too Forward) vii
Intro: In Bed With the Muse ix
Act 1 3
    Sonnet 8 5
    Sonnet 45 6
    Sonnet 11PM 7
    Sonnet 69 8
    Sonnet 666 9
    Sonnet 32° 10
    Sonnet 411 11
    Sonnet 13 12
    Sonnet 6" 13
    Sonnet -1 14
Act 2 15
    Sonnet 1-800 17
    Sonnet 8x10 18
    Sonnet 12.11.15 19
    Sonnet 6E 20
    Sonnet 2^n 21
    Sonnet ¾ 22
    Sonnet 10-4 23
    Sonnet 06801 24
Act 2A 25
    Sonnet 18k 27
    Sonnet 370 B.C. 28
    Sonnet 33 1/3 29
    Sonnet 24/7 30
    Sonnet $18.99 31
    Sonnet 917-589-9XXX 32
    Sonnet <2 33
Act II 35
    Sonnet IIX or Sonnet VIII 37
    Sonnet i 38
    Sonnet X+Y 39

Sonnet L	40
Sonnet B^2	41
Sonnet *Seventeen* magazine	42
Sonnet X=X	43
Act IV	45
Sonnet Infinity	47
Sonnet Pi	48
Sonnet Gazillion	49
Sonnet Phi	50
Sonnet Tau	51
Sonnet 0	52
Sonnet Ø	53
Sonnet #	54
A Page of Thank You	55
Acknowledgements	56
About the Author	57

Foreword (But Not Too Forward)

A love affair is like a new puppy. So much trouble! So much fun!

It keeps you up late. It makes you miss work. It demands to go out, it whines when you leave. It stains the sheets, chews up your books, pulls at the leash.

A love affair is young, joyful, and proud. It plays in the park; it nuzzles your hand. It thrills to your voice; it jumps at the door. It curls up by your side. It adores you.

Infinity Standing Up tells the messy, rowdy, off-again/on-again story of a passionate love affair in the form of 40 generally Shakespearean sonnets, each one a square box of 14 lines, 10 beats to a line, rhyming true to the form: abab, cdcd, efef, gg. Each one is a meticulously crafted dog-crate for the untrained puppy of love.

Of course these are not the first sonnets to attempt the task of wrestling a doggish passion into order. Poet Drew Pisarra joins a long line of lovers who have used the sonnet form to rebuild walls and repair roofs after a hurricane of love and loss. These sonnets are Shakespearean, in form and also spirit, in their celebration of the lustful male body, in their evocation of a dark young rival, in their hope and wonder and ultimately bitter betrayal and loss.

The editors of *The Norton Anthology of Poetry* call the sonnet form the "best example of how rhyme and meter can provide the imagination not with a prison but with a theater." A jumping young dog can't spend its life in a cage, no matter how charmingly constructed. And the kitchen counter of a first fuck can turn into a Sleep Number mattress when the kids come along.

So like all good sonnets, the energy and force of these poems pushes against the box of the form. The title itself expresses this tension. *Infinity Standing Up*: Infinity is by definition without boundaries, but when it stands up it becomes 8, a square box of 2's. There's lots of play with numbers and math in these poems, but most of the energy comes from an enthusiastic vulgarity of language and image, like the dog that sniffs your crotch or won't stop humping your leg. You might find it troublesome, but you admire its push. And the clever play of rhyme and image in these poems is alive and free, a puppy running off the leash.

The very first poem of the collection, "Sonnet 8," is a perfect example of both the beautiful cage and the animal body panting inside. The speaker imagines himself eaten up by his lover, swallowed up "inside your mouth feet first." The image moves along in a pulsing peristaltic wave, through lips, throat, lung, heart, ribs, diaphragm, hips, and kidneys, accompanied by digestive sound effects, a slurp, a burp, until the last line, inspired and inevitable: "This love's a gas so shoot me out your butt."

From this exuberant wind-tossed beginning, the poems travel fast through changing weather: almost immediately the humid tangle of sheets suggested by "I'm 32 in Celsius, not Fahrenheit," becomes "Naked I shiv-/ered." Summer to winter, the seasons change, tides rise and fall. The affair ends and begins again, compulsive and resigned, bitter and dry.

I'm giving away the ending, and the ending is sad. Ultimately, the love affair is over. The joyful fart of "Sonnet 8" becomes a wistful sigh.

But the poems!

Here they are.

Mare Davis, Ph. D.

Intro: In Bed With the Muse

I can't honestly pretend that I've never written a love poem before. Of course I have. But an entire series of them? No, this was something new. I suppose breaking up helped. As did getting back together again. And breaking up again. If we'd ever really broken up. If we'd ever really been together. But what started off as a simple expression of affection, passion, lust, joy, what to call it at any given moment I couldn't tell… regularly switched into a less-than-simple expression of frustration, disappointment, confusion, hurt or an all-around ache. I'll admit sometimes I went off the rails. Why not? I was weary of the rails and the day to day. But what was going on here in the after hours? What did it mean? What did he mean? Was he it? Was it love? Was love sex? Does that have meaning too? Even when it's meaningless? Everything seemed so loaded, even rarified questions like: Why are sonnets always numbered? What's in a number? And what if a sonnet were numbered infinity or pi or as a fraction or the price of a couple of a tacos? How would that affect the way we read it or what it might mean? What would it signify? What if the sonnet had a longer line? What if the rhyme scheme got a tweak or faltered? Could I write a sonnet a la Petrarch? How about one by way of Gertrude Stein? And would I sleep with him again? No. But then I did. No. But then I did again. Until I didn't. By then the series was almost done. I still had a few things to confess but really, my audience had exited the room. What he left behind was a book. Although I wrote it, he made it happen. And I'm going to ignore that recent sext.

Drew Pisarra

INFINITY STANDING UP

Act 1

Sonnet 8

I'd like to climb inside your mouth feet first
to tickle toes upon your teeth and tongue
then pull you by your lips up like a skirt
'til my right thigh is touching your left lung.
I'll sayonara to that sky of blue
as down your throat I go (sound cue one: slurp)
to wrestle with your heart midst all that's you.
Then once I triumph, sound cue two: a burp.
I'd play a tune on xylophonic ribs
and make your diaphragm my trampoline
to spring me to that spot near grinding hips
where kidneys dance in pairs like jumping beans.
Devour me! Think me not some crazy nut.
This love's a gas so shoot me out your butt.

Sonnet 45

the lyrics go something like yeah, yeah, yeah
while the drum goes chitch underwater cunk cunk
and the singer goes yeah babe yeah yeah yeah
then electric guitar wangs wah wah funk
and you're holding me close so close so close
'til the chorus goes ew wah ew wah ew
and I can't hear the words: yeah yeah at most
'cause you're kissing me and I'm kissing you
when the tempo picks up we won't slow down
when the rhythm gets funky we'll do the same
we'll join in for verses sung wrong and loud
and scream 'til the world thinks we're insane
that stupid refrain again and again
yeah yeah yeah please play us that song again

Sonnet 11PM

Pajamas are a form of formal wear, the tux
of the bedroom, the suit of the boudoir. I own
two pair: one, a blue Mao suit; the other, a luxe
cliché. You know, you've stripped me of both. Had I known
pajamas were lingerie, I'd have insisted
you wear mine sooner. You see, I couldn't care less
that on you, the pants ride high and my waistband gives
so the snaps unsnap... My dear, I fetishize this.
If clothes make the man, then jammies make the lover.
Dressed or undressed. Tops and bottoms. You're well-paired
with me. I'll take you wherever and whenever,
whatever you wear. In the end, you'll end up bare.
Neither of us will honor this costume of sleep.
I see on it your face: first the goat, then the sheep.

Sonnet 69

What a cunning way to depict a sex
act! What a visual symbol for such
sensual play! Oh, what wise intellects
first saw in these digits the way to touch
on the frankly risqué! And like the two
tail-chasing fish in the house of Pisces,
the top of a half-stripped Phillips head screw,
this yin-yang icon of carnal vices
is an Escher-like sketch telling us what
to do. Easier than Kama Sutra
or a range of derangement for the butt,
this mouth-to-south is the ne plus ultra
for those who find delight in give and get.
As above, so below, this tête-à-tête.

Sonnet 666

You must be the Devil himself for how
else to explain this freewheeling desire
that's made me the pervert that I am now,
a wanton minion with a need for fire
in human form. A month ago, Satan
was the big, fat joke that suddenly came
into existence. Now sex is a freaking
addiction that's as wack as crack cocaine.
Well, he who French kisses the forkéd tongue
must therefore obey its screwy commands
like lick and suck, swallow, beg. I've become
undone by more than I can stand here in
this unmade bed of your customized hell
where needing's a sin. God, you sin damn well.

Sonnet 32°

I'll be the first to admit I'm cold. Yet the truth
of the matter is this: You grow bored when I'm nice.
You're quite aroused by a standoffish attitude.
You get your rocks off by chewing Freudian ice.
I told you point blank, I'd never say no. But oh!
How you cooled to Pavlovian yes. Nowadays
I turn the flame down low so when we meet you'll know
you're the source of the heat, I guess. Wise men say,
"Many's the fool who mistakes frosty for frigid."
You've said so yourself while half sneering, half smirking.
I keep my own face blank. I try not to fidget.
Only Kinsey himself could spot lust like this lurking.
I don't care if this role-playing is wrong or right:
I'm 32 in Celsius, not Fahrenheit.

Sonnet 411

In thrillers, the secrets cause all the grief
for what we withhold surely leads to doom.
It's the constant potential of relief
we sweep under threadbare rugs in our rooms
of this cheap motel on a rundown street.
Amid dead payphones and the stink of smoke,
we flash fake IDs every time we meet
for rewound confessions replayed as jokes.
There's so much omitted, so much sidestepped
so much that never quite passes our lips.
What I never learn is what I'll never forget.
You've touched me without leaving fingerprints.
Now half-truths smolder in a chipped ashtray
but what you mean to me, I couldn't say.

Sonnet 13

I shall hereby pinpoint the exact moment when whatever we had was irreparably ruined, decisively broken, damaged for good. I could feel our separation in my bones, as if a poison had entered the marrow like chemotherapy gone awry. Your words were noisome to me since you pretended the violence had not occurred or could be overlooked, dismissed, ignored. Naked I shivered with rage, not really recovering so much as nursing a wound you'd given me without regret whilst you sat staring out the window at a dying star.

Sonnet 6"

Hey shlong, listen up. Hey penis, pay attention.
Pecker! Turn your unblinking eye over here.
Oh, thick-headed prick, oh tool of no pretension,
oh wood that could, and dick shaped like a can of beer.
I have ogled and gagged. I have ridden such cock.
I now testify to shafts fat and thin that assume
import for an hour then become standard stock.
Some were memorable, some not. But as to you
and yours divine which had given me such pleasure,
I had hoped to make it mine. Yet I had to let
it go. Neither you nor your manhood would measure
up to my far-flung desires. So what don't you get?
Like your dick, our love didn't prove to be that deep
but even shallow love lost can feel bittersweet.

Sonnet -1

I'd be lying if I said this old heart didn't
ache, that my nights aren't restless, that a dream
didn't fade. I'm not wailing, more like sighing. Isn't
that a softer grief, appropriate in scale? It seems
preposterous to say, I wish your loving me
would've lasted longer, had been more than passing
fancy, that our romance hadn't ended with me
getting dumped for that beauty from central casting:
Younger, taller, smarter, with a full set of teeth.
As for me, I'm losing hair and height and brain cells.
I've had a tooth pulled, deadening nerves underneath.
I'll pretend, age is a number. Oh sheesh. Oh well.
In a weird way I gave what I thought was my best,
then discovered what I thought was the best was less.

Act 2

Sonnet 1-800

In 1989, my friend Mary
worked for the sex line 1-800-DUCK
where she more often took calls from scary
coke addicts than horn-dogs lacking the pluck
to approach girls in nightclubs. Back then
I smirked at the dialed-up idiocy
of convos billing jerks by the second
for not-so-hot hotline intimacy.
Yet where are we now? With our lovelorn apps
(Grindr, Tinder, Tingle, Scruff, and Diskreet)
that spell out longing via finger taps,
our hammered-out virtual meet-and-greets.
Goodbye, chatterbox – so lonely, so high.
Hey, emoticon heart... r u nearby?

Sonnet 8x10

Never date an actor my mother warned,
not that she'd ever dated one herself,
but artsy types have sketchy mental health
and life is to be lived and not performed.
As proof, she cited her sad marriage to
my father who was frequently mistook
for Henry Winkler. That alike, his look!
For her the look was everything. Tis true!
Life is an act, she said, with roles pre-set
but not quite posed and we ought always be
as inconspicuous as possible.
Despite her words, I favor extroverts,
because I like the rebel quality
of men who thrive in lives of "show and tell."

Sonnet 12.11.15

The day we met, we talked of Fassbinder,
The Story of O, the dying of bees…
That very night you showed me your Tinder
profile as if in some way it would please
me to see you seducing the city
at large. And it did. It still does. I like
your broad appeal, your versatility,
your hourly refusal to be typed,
and I'm aware I too often limit
myself. That Winter, polyamorous
dalliances were beyond my scope. Shit,
sleeping around didn't feel glamorous
that unseasonably warm December.
Am I someone you even remember?

Sonnet 6E

How dare you ask my apartment number
as if you hadn't been here 34
times, as if we hadn't spent those late nights
kissing and humping each other dumber,
as if my address somehow slipped your
mind, as if you'd forgotten those six flights
you'll have to climb. Again. I bet I'll smell
liquor on your breath, likely taste the one
hundred proof sweated out of your armpit
and neck not long after I hear the bell
letting me know it's time to buzz you in.
But as for the next time, should you forget:
6 is for half-dozen, E is for egg.
Get your ass up here before I renege.

Sonnet 2^n

to mend every rend, to test our intent,
to stay or to leave, and with each new split
to rehash the verse or rewrite what's meant
by too much or too little; sheesh, the shit
we might admit to basically boggles
the mind; even so, we know to wait, to breathe,
to listen, to hush, to bend, to toggle
between compromise and integrity
as the depths to which we plummet surface
whenever we're eye to eye, skin to skin,
nose to nose because of my two-purposed
brain that craves out freedom and a way in;
but to quip that one plus one equals two
is to subtract infinities from you

Sonnet ¾

We were both in the park this afternoon,
a dog was off leash, you were not alone,
your boyfriend was with you, I felt marooned
especially after you'd mouthed "Hello."

The time before that? In fact, no better.
Your heads peeped into my favorite café
to spoil my meal then vanish away.
Afterwards, I found food on my sweater

and shirt. It left a stain that would not lift.
I tried. Well, some things cannot be wiped clean
like that time his smiling face popped up on
your iPhone's smashed screen. It went by so swift,

his face – to me unknown, though not unseen
if soon deleted. Soon, I too was gone.

Sonnet 10-4

When the end first came, I wrote you a poem,
then I wrote another when it ended
again. Our breakup just kept on going
and going as if we had intended
to never be friends. It was lovers or
nothing, good-for-nothing at that. My heart
broke more often than cheap dinnerware. Your
crack about how our romance came in spurts
was the double entendre that made me
laugh 'til it hurt. I could write you more rhymes
of what I'll miss, of our urbanity,
of chances lost, of verse undone. At times,
your going seems Shakespearean. Alack!
You stole my heart but I don't want you back.

Sonnet 06801

I've seen your body but never your face,
stared at your cock but not into your eyes.
I've read your thoughts in a virtual space.
As to your voice, it'll be a surprise
'cause I'm ready to travel to Bethel.
That is, of course, if your invite still stands
and I don't sound as cracked as an eggshell.
I've got those directions you gave, in hand:
You're the next to last stop on Metro North's
Danbury branch of the New Haven line.
I've got your contact info and so forth.
All I need is an exact date and time.
Once I get there we'll decide what to do.
Introductions first: I'm Drew. Who are you?

Act 2A

Sonnet 18k

You stand naked at my desk with your back
to me. Yet even when viewed from the rear,
so to speak, you can throw me out of whack.
I do my best to make my thinking clear
but lust has its own kinky logic and
soon my mind races back, seeking random
facts picked up from long-forgotten science
class, like how the skin is a sex organ
in a sci-fi kind of way or gold is
a soft metal graded for purity.
I see how such knowledge applies to this
body, my shrine of biochemistry.
Your flesh is warmer and kinder than brass
so why shouldn't I kiss that Golden Ass?

Sonnet 370 B.C.

There's a cautionary line in *Phaedrus*
by Plato: "Love is a mental disease."
The larger work too instills an unease
with dialogue pointedly about us;
the older man (with a younger muse)
I blindly recoil from Socrates
slyly noting he unfailingly sees
the beauteous limitations of youth
as a source inspiration. And now
I know even Ancient Greeks once suffered
from mid-life crises which now prove tougher
to weather once symptoms are pointed out.
Some things we sorely wish were never said.
Equally true: What's read can't be unread.

Sonnet 33 1/3

We never had one single song we called
our own though you would sing me melodies --
strange, made-up punk rock ditties that enthralled
me with their amorous atrocities.
You sang of queers who fucked in Nazi camps,
of eggs averting birth to save the world,
of horror films where killers wore no pants
so they could run free. And though not the worst
part of our on-again off-again ways,
the latest loss of you stings me anew
as if a rare LP, worn by replays,
was lost or scratched beyond repair. It's true
I know these songs by heart, sides A and B,
but who can play a solo symphony?

Sonnet 24/7

I've tasted another's sweat on your tongue
and licked off a stranger's spit from your ear
o'erheard your sleeping voice and been stung
by an unknown name of no one near here.
Who am I to complain? What am I to do?
When doesn't affection come with a sting?
Why shouldn't I settle for less of you
instead of much more of a dingaling?
You gift me hours, I savor each minute.
You show up one night then you're gone for days.
Months pass, links weaken. Then we're back at it
in the shower or squeezed onto my chaise.
In my dreams, we're together 'round the clock.
This room knows different: Tickety tock.

Sonnet $18.99

You wouldn't even let me treat you to tacos
because you equated me buying you dinner
with dating and so we watched YouTube videos
before sex then chatted like two shy beginners
post-boink, our eyes cast downwards or staring out
into the dark, unseeing. You spoke of the Mexican
novel for some reason. I wanted to talk about
feelings, briefly albeit. Then we fucked again.
All that ended with the following text last night:
"My boyfriend arrives tomorrow from Caracas.
Are you free now?" It took me six hours to reply:
"Love deeply, not widely, in both Americas."
I wanted to blame you for making me feel cheap
but I knew you weren't single. So who's the creep?

Sonnet 917-589-9XXX

u texted me on xmas 2 wish me
merry I texted u later 2 wish
u back rashly I sexted u happy
come NEW YEAR!! admittedly hornyish
my resolve now gone slack not looking not
not looking ears pealed 4 a ping & ping
me u did 10 minutes later we're hot
& heavy in my hall & you're doing
that thing you do those things you do we do
every time we get together but
it/s been quite awhile so the old felt new
well not quite new & frankly not quite hot
until you fell asleep & snored & snored
& held me in your arms as I grew bored

Sonnet <2

You stood at the corner of Flatbush and Dean Street.
I stood right beside you. The light had turned red.
You stood facing forward. I saw you discreetly,
completely, but then later, I wished that I'd said:
You know what? I hate you. You hear me? I mean it.
I admit I once cared but I no longer do.
Instead at the corner of Flatbush and Dean Street
I blurted *Hello there. Oh, I'm fine. How are you?*
You asked me dull questions. My answers? So boring.
The couple beside us at Flatbush and Dean
were clueless to the drama so clearly unfolding.
Then again, no one really hears what silence means.
Finally, the light turned green. You walked. I held back
as if suddenly engulfed by a sidewalk crack.

Act II

Sonnet IIX or Sonnet VIII

Eyed lick two climes inns hide door mount feed furs,
two tackled toads (hizzoner seething tons);
thin bullion-buyer lit supplies ash-curd
still mire height thy hiss dodging gore lifelong.
Hail, sigh or not a doodad's guy half-brew,
his browner 'fro dyed cobalt-cute once slur.
Due west nitwit, pure harmest doth have stew.
Ten onesies, try on. Zounds! Glue do what verb
hype prayer dooming silo phone encrypts,
hand major dial pram nigh dram pore lean
you spindly tube-tapped spotter's grinning gifts
weird kids' knees dent tin bear-like chum pansies.
Thee hourly stinky knobs, sun-crazed, see nubs,
dislodging cares for chewy outer buds.

Sonnet i

i've become so small since seeing you or
more like from how little you see me now
and how not seeing you makes me feel for
you see i see myself more now in how
i am perceived than how i came to be
this way and how wee our we has become
and how that came to pass this me not me
no me myself and I the total sum
a some less thing or a thing less same than
i would want it but it is what it is
and what it is isn't and you're not and
i can't and we were but we aren't this
thing that i miss that never truly was
but i wish wishing made it so because

Sonnet X+Y

In the film, Victor Frankenstein creates a mate
to wed his monster. She's a fright-wigged she-devil
who cares little for muscles. For her, what rates
is a pretty face. In Mary Shelley's novel
of ideas, that mail-order bride barely appears.
Disappointment belongs to the men who flee North
to Alaska, each overcome by guilt and fear.
No doubt, I've muddled the basic plot. Of course,
you could argue that *Frankenstein* is a thwarted
bromance, a tale of two doomed souls unable to
mend the rifts that come when desire drifts. What started
as a bold experiment failed. Now what to do?
I will never be the man you want me to be.
But I am still something. Please think creatively.

Sonnet L

This bed has a headboard made of metal,
a mattress with at least one broken spring.
It looks quite stolen from a hospital
in a county prison or some sad thing
cast off by an orphanage. It looks used.
It is that. Old too. Half a century.
It can squeak one awake during a snooze
or creak out scores for acts of lechery.
That's what it's been doing the last half-hour,
making rhythmic noise like two panicked mice,
or a voice of steel, that's better, crying out
the need, the need, the need, oh how nice,
the need the need the need. That's what I hear
on sheets that look clean until you come near.

Sonnet B²

B is for brains and beat-up bifocals,
black and blue elbows and bad overbites,
brooding brown eyes and biceps like baseballs.
B is da bomb! So where were you last night?
Blah-bitty-blah-blah. I've heard that before -
the best laid bullshit this side of Beijing:
Keep blaming that buddy from Baltimore,
and I'll bash in your Buick. Stop babbling.
You beat 'round the bush. You've burnt every bridge.
You're bruising and blighting beyond beyond.
Now bye-bye be-yotch I bitterly bid.
The billionth botch-up will break any bond.
The best was basically what came before.
Bygones are bygones. Go bless the back door.

Sonnet *Seventeen* magazine

Halfway through existence, I sense the next
guy you fall head over heels for will be
a well-built but headless torso who'll sext
you night and day about his buns of steel.
He'll get *Men's Health*, and not the *New Yorker*
and it's you, not him, who'll acknowledge how
shallow you've become. Shallow! Why talk of
something deep when "deep" causes giggles now?
What's deep or dumb for a middle-aged creep
have to do with you? Each mirror you pass
is glazed with steam. Each nightmare that you sleep
through is a rewrite of yesterday's trash.
Awake or unconscious, you're full of crap
and if you were here… Well, here comes the slap.

Sonnet X=X

I'm going to pretend he was twenty
nine and not twenty eight since he told me
he was ringing in his birthday when he
came over to my place at three yes three
in the morning. That's frankly the middle
of the night. I heard when his LYFT car stopped
outside my building then watched him fiddle
the front door's one lock with a key I'd dropped
from way up high. From my peephole, I saw
him leave the elevator then look my
way. (I'm at the end of the hall.) I pawed
at his lithe body without caring. I
knew all along he wasn't you, dear ex,
but he was there for me and sex is sex.

Act IV

Sonnet Infinity

On the subway this morning, I spotted your hair
on some other man's head: unexpectedly unwashed.
It gave pause. So weird. How'd it get there? And who cares?
I had to look away and fast but then I caught
your eyes staring at me from an infant nearby.
Don't get me wrong. I'm not so deranged as to say
that baby's baby browns were your two peerless eyes
transplanted. It's just, throughout my surreal day,
I saw your legs, your arms, your neck reattached to
various torsos while your lips, your nose, your ears
landed magically on face after face. Who's
to say what lies hidden inside some stranger's jeans?
You are so on my mind even when you're not here
that wherever I go, parts of you reappear.

Sonnet Pi

"Love never ends." Or so you contend. "Well neither
does pi" is my curt reply. "Affections divide
till the end of time." Basically, you can either
come to terms with that cold truth or chase the big lie.
It's silly to frame love as unending pleasure
or assign it a stature mathematic in scope.
It's easier to square a circle, than to measure
one heart's full capacity so while you may hope
to convince me there's magic in threes, three being you
me and he, that triangle "we" sounds like a mess
of self-serving logic that will never prove true.
Polyamory has always struck me as less
than the sum of its parts. This is the lesson learned
by one who tried to be "open" then got burned.

Sonnet Gazillion

Does anyone else find it funny or
queer that the God of Love is an infant,
a chubby trickster-toddler with a pair
of wings, a pesky airborne brat who can't
or won't stop shooting those countless arrows
from the sky, arrows that rain down on us
from on high in numbers too great to count?
None of us will escape. Not one of us
will really try for each of us wishes,
not-so-secretly, that some well-aimed shaft
will pierce our heart, or if it misses
that, grazes our ass. Cupid likes to laugh
in the deadpan face of propriety.
Does anyone else find Eros funny?

Sonnet Phi

Why articulate an abstract idea
so divorced from quantifiable facts
when I can calculate what was real
and what's not, old friend. No, I won't retract
my foolish belief that our feelings were
deep, so deep they defied all convention.
Were we lovers? Soul mates? Something greater,
less twee? We kissed in multi-dimensions
and redefined our relationship as
"two parts brain paired with one part emotion."
If it didn't add up, still I let it pass,
settling for far less than devotion.
Our now-gone thing was a false equation
based on mistruths and a cruel evasion.

Sonnet Tau

God knows I have tried to compute what you
mean to me as if such things could translate
into mathematics like the value
of A plus B over A equals A
divided by B where A stands for All,
B for Better; but sentiments refuse
being quantified. Love's conceptual
not numerical. Anyway folks use
Phi, not Tau, for the golden ratio,
and no one but a heartbroken math geek
would reference Greek letters such as Rho
which is worth but a third of Tau. To speak
of this loss is to speak of subtraction.
It's not complex. I'm a simple fraction.

Sonnet 0

Some dude should pen a love poem to you, a guy
not waylaid by your kisses, a man who stays cool
to your heated touch and won't melt so much or cry
tears of pleasure during sex like a goddamned fool.
I'll never paint portraits of you nor sculpt your like,
nor bake you the cake that would take the cake nor grow
you a rose with your name, for your nose. You know why?
'cause every time I begin, I retreat so…
Let betters compose better love songs or screen-write
rom-coms that are romans a clef with *you* as muse.
As for me, I'm not vying to be Mr. Right
or worse yet the one that got away. You may choose
whom you wish. Let *him* coin a heartfelt, dime-store rhyme.
I wish I could write it but I can't. Not this time.

Sonnet Ø

It will be over soon. It will soon be
over. It will be over. It's over.
It is. It is over. It's so very
over, it's over over. I'm over
it. Or very soon. I so am. I'm past
over, past past, over the past. I am.
I am past the past. I'm so past the past
I've overpassed. I'm passed over. And I'm
not passing over the being passed over,
the very soon-to-be passed in the past.
The soon-to-be not-to-be? That's over.
The over way too soon? That too will pass.
In other words: So very soon, there's me.
Just me, me, me, me oh my oh me.

Sonnet

When my therapist asked whether you had
any kinks I told her no and you know
I tell her everything, both good and bad,
not that she's one to pass judgment although
there was that one time when but I digress…
When my therapist asked if you'd any
kinks, I told her no, not really, unless
she factored in *ours* as *we* had many.
She sighed then waited as therapists do.
Emboldened by silence, I decided
to tell her ALL be it odd, wrong, or crude
but then she interrupted me and said
I should wait before I'd even begun
because this afternoon's session was done.

A Page of Thank You

Much of these poems can be attributed to a single muse while a subset of them must also be credited in part to the generous encouragement of editor Regie Cabico. That said, a number of people also deserve the kind nod of appreciation including Lynn Ann Kister, my cowboy poet pen pal for keeping me on track; Angie Morrill, my long-distance confidante and confessor; Cynthia Chimienti, my fellow Sagittarian investigator of the Id; Jen Ziegler who heard the running narrative in 3.3 mile bursts; Jen Lam and Helen Zelon for always nudging me back to Shakespeare; Mare Davis, a dearly beloved book buddy; and Molly Gross, my lifelong friend who has often held a flashlight to point the way. Thank you also to Anna Girvan, Joan Larkin, Lisa Ann Markuson, Kate Lutzner, and Diane Mehta for their thoughtful responses to the manuscript as well as Gisburg, Linda Manning, Pamela Booker, Karen Hudes, and Jessica Branch for fueling my writing outside poetry. No less important were Clara Zwirble and Kelly Maloni for their uninterrupted boosterism which I, for one, will never undervalue. Last but not least, thank you to Sasha Sinclair whose generosity of spirit is legion.

Acknowledgements

Grateful acknowledgment is made to the following publications in which these poems initially appeared: *Algebra of Owls*: "Sonnet 1-800," "Sonnet 917-589-9XXX," and "Sonnet B^2"; *Chantwood*: "Sonnet Infinity"; *City Brink*: "Sonnet 18k" and "Sonnet X=X"; *Clementine Unbound*: "Sonnet 12.11.15"; *Hawai`i Pacific Review*: "Sonnet X+Y"; *KYSO Flash*: "Sonnet <2"; *Poydras Review*: "Sonnet $18.99"; *Route 7 Review*: "Sonnet Pi" (originally published under the title "Sonnet 3.14159"); *Super Stoked*: "Sonnet 69," "Sonnet 6"," and "Sonnet X=X"; *THAT Literary Review*: "Sonnet 11PM" and "Sonnet 32°"; *The Blue Nib*: "Sonnet 6E," "Sonnet i," and "Sonnet Phi"; *The Voices Project*: "Sonnet -1"; *The Wild Word*: "Sonnet 10/4"; *Third Wednesday*: "Sonnet 666"; and *Vine Leaves Literary Journal*: "Sonnet 0."

About the Author

Aside from his work as a poet (which includes the chapbooks *Untitled & Other Poems* and *Religion, Anatomy, Catastrophe*), Drew Pisarra once toured his monologues *Queer Notions*, *Fickle*, and *The Gospel According to Saint Genet* around the country and even had a ventriloquist act (*Singularly Grotesque*, commissioned by the Portland Institute for Contemporary Art) but has since retired from the world of dummies. His short story collection *Publick Spanking* was published by Future Tense some time ago. More recently as part of the installation art duo Saint Flashlight (with Molly Gross), he's been finding inventive ways to get poetry into public spaces.

Photo of author with his movie marquee haiku in Brooklyn by Molly Gross

www.ingramcontent.com/pod-product-compliance
Lightning Source LLC
Chambersburg PA
CBHW072024060426
42449CB00034B/2161